Welcome to Local Government in Ontario

in English

Ontario
Ministry of Municipal Affairs
John Eakins, Minister

1988
ISBN: 0-7729-3889-X

Published by the Ministry of Municipal Affairs
Printed by the Queen's Printer for Ontario, Province of Ontario,
Toronto, Canada.

WELCOME TO LOCAL GOVERNMENT IN ONTARIO

Acknowledgements

A special thanks to the many people in community agencies, local government and Ontario Government Ministries for their assistance, suggestions, revisions and support.

Please note

The information in this book is up-to-date as of January, 1988. For more current information, please contact the appropriate agency.

Distribution

This publication is available free to Ontario newcomers, their teachers and counsellors. Immigrant aid agencies, schools and other non-profit organizations serving newcomers may obtain copies to distribute to adult newcomers by contacting:

Ontario Ministry of Municipal Affairs
11th floor, 777 Bay Street
Toronto, Ontario M5G 2E5
Telephone (416) 585-7201

Additional Copies

Additional copies may be purchased at $2.50 per copy from:

Ontario Government Bookstore
880 Bay Street
Toronto, Ontario M7A 1N8
Telephone: (416) 965-2054.

Outside Toronto, write to:

Publication Services Section
5th floor, 880 Bay Street
Toronto, Ontario M7A 1N8
Telephone: (416) 965-2054
Toll-free long distance 1-800-268-7540
In northwestern Ontario, 0-Zenith 67200

MINISTER'S MESSAGE

Welcome to Ontario!

The Ministry of Municipal Affairs is pleased to provide this handbook to assist newcomers to learn about local government and the many services it provides.

People from many lands around the world have played an important role in making Ontario's municipalities enjoyable places to live and work. We look forward to the continued participation of newcomers in the life of their communities and the province.

I invite all new residents to participate in local government, and I wish you all the best as you begin your new life in Ontario.

John Eakins
Minister of Municipal Affairs

TABLE OF CONTENTS

ACKNOWLEDGEMENTS ii

MINISTER'S MESSAGE iv

INTRODUCTION 1

GOVERNMENT IN ONTARIO 2

The Federal Government 2
The Provincial Government 2
Local Government 3

MUNICIPALITIES 4

Local Municipalities 4
Counties and Regions 4
Metropolitan Toronto 4
Improvement Districts 5
Municipal Councils 5
How Does Council Govern? 6
Bringing a Matter to Council's Attention 7

LOCAL BOARDS AND COMMISSIONS 7

BOARDS OF EDUCATION 7

PUBLIC UTILITIES COMMISSIONS 8

LOCAL GOVERNMENT ELECTIONS

How Are Municipal Councillors Elected? . . . 8
What About Metro Toronto Council? . . . 9
How is The Head of Council Elected? . . . 9
What About County Councils? . . . 9
What About Regional Councils? . . . 10
How Are School Boards Elected? . . . 10
How Are Public Utilities Commissions Elected? . . . 11
When Are Local Elections Held? . . . 11
Who Can Vote in the Elections? . . . 11
Who Can Be a Candidate? . . . 11
Where to Vote . . . 12
Who Runs the Elections? . . . 12
When Are the Election Results Known? . . . 12

LOCAL GOVERNMENT FUNDING . . . 13

Property Taxes . . . 13
Assessing the Property . . . 13
Setting the Mill Rate . . . 15
Calculating Your Taxes . . . 16
Paying Your Property Taxes . . . 16
Interim Tax Bill . . . 16
Instalments . . . 16
What Happens If Taxes Are Not Paid? . . . 18
Tax Grants for Senior Citizens . . . 18

GUIDE TO LOCAL GOVERNMENT SERVICES . . . 19

THE MUNICIPAL CLERK'S OFFICE . . . 19

Business Licences . . . 20

POLICE PROTECTION . . . 20

If You Need Help . . . 21

FIRE PROTECTION . . . 21

AMBULANCE SERVICES 22

DIAL 911 22

TRANSPORTATION SERVICES

Public Transportation 22
Metro Toronto 23
Services for the Handicapped 23
GO Transit 24

PARKING 24

Meter Parking 24
Parking Fines 25
Parking Permits for the Handicapped 25

ROAD AND SIDEWALK MAINTENANCE 25

SNOW REMOVAL 26

STREET LIGHTING 26

GARBAGE COLLECTION AND DISPOSAL

Garbage Collection 27
Recycling 27
Burning Garbage 28
Where To Get More Information 28

RECREATION AND CULTURE 28

Parks 28
Libraries 29

SOCIAL SERVICES

General Welfare Assistance 29
Special Assistance and Supplementary Aid 30
Other Financial and Employment Assistance 31
Child Care 31
Children's Aid Societies 32
Services for the Elderly 32
Aids for Independence 32
Elderly Persons' Centres 32
Homes for the Aged 32

PUBLIC HEALTH SERVICES 33

ANIMAL CONTROL

Licensing 34
Exotic Pets 34
Lost Pets 34
Humane Care 34
Animal Bites 35

LAND USE PLANNING

What Is Land Use Planning? 35
The Zoning By-law 35
How Does the Zoning By-law Affect You? 36
How is a Zoning By-law Changed? 36
What If You Want Your Zoning Changed? 36
What Right Of Appeal Do You Have? 37
What If All You Need Is a Minor Change in the By-law? 37
Land Severance 38

BUILDING

Building Permits 38
How To Apply for a Building Permit 39
Building Inspections 39
Building Demolition 40
Property Standards By-laws 40
Signs, Awnings, Fences and Hedges 40

EDUCATION 41

Elementary School 41
Secondary School 41
Enrolling Your Child in School 42
School Bus Service 42
Language Instruction 42
Special Programs 42
Adult Education 43

ELECTRICITY

Your Electricity Bill 43
Advice on Saving Energy 43

WATER AND SEWER SERVICES 44

Having Your Meter Read 45

WHERE TO FIND OUT MORE 46

GLOSSARY 47

INTRODUCTION

Night and day, every day of the year, the services provided by local government are working for you.

From the minute you turn on the light in the morning until you turn it off again at night, and even while you sleep, local government plays an important part in your daily life.

Think about the water that provides you with a hot shower; the electricity for your radio; the buses that take adults to work and children to school; the school itself; the roads and sidewalks you use to go shopping; and the library, park or arena you visit on your way home. Police and fire protection, garbage collection, help for people in need, and many other community services are provided by local government.

Because local government touches all of us in so many ways, it is important that we understand how it works. This book gives a brief introduction to local government in Ontario. It tells you about the services local government provides, and how you can obtain them, and it discusses how you can take part in making the decisions that affect your community.

GOVERNMENT IN ONTARIO

There are three levels of government in Ontario:

- the Government of Canada (federal government);
- the Government of Ontario (provincial government); and
- local government (municipalities, school boards, public utilities commissions, and local boards and commissions).

Each level of government is responsible for certain services.

The Federal Government

The federal government is responsible for matters that affect all of Canada, for example:

- national defence
- citizenship
- foreign policy
- national economic policy
- currency

The Provincial Government

The Government of Ontario is responsible for matters which affect the province, for example:

- highways
- social services
- health care
- industrial growth
- protecting the environment

Local Government

Local government is responsible for matters that affect the local area, for example:

- protecting homes and businesses from fire
- providing schools
- operating municipal libraries
- building parks and recreation facilities
- planning new neighbourhoods

Why is local government responsible for so many important services? Because local government is close to the people it serves. It knows the local community's needs and how to meet those needs.

Local government is composed of several parts:

- municipalities
- local boards and commissions
- school boards
- public utilities commissions

Each of these will be discussed in turn.

MUNICIPALITIES

There are 839 municipalities in Ontario. No two are exactly the same. Municipalities range in size from Metropolitan Toronto – with more than two million people – to Cockburn Island Township – which has only two permanent residents. Two-thirds of the people in Ontario live in the province's 50 largest municipalities. The population of most municipalities is quite small. About 600 municipalities in the province have fewer than 5,000 people.

Local Municipalities

Depending on its size, a local municipality may be called a city (large municipalities), a town (medium) or a township or village (small). Whatever its name, your local municipality provides most of the municipal services you receive.

Counties and Regions

It may be more efficient to provide some services over an area larger than an individual local municipality. For this reason, most local municipalities in Southern Ontario are grouped into counties (mainly in rural areas) or regional municipalities (mainly in urban areas). Regional municipalities are often called "regions." For example, the Cities of Brampton and Mississauga and the Town of Caledon are all part of the Regional Municipality of Peel. Similarly, the County of Oxford includes the City of Woodstock, the Towns of Ingersoll and Tillsonburg and the Townships of Blandford-Blenheim, East Zorra-Tavistock, Norwich, South West Oxford and Zorra.

Counties and regions work with local municipalities to provide a range of municipal services.

Metropolitan Toronto

Metropolitan Toronto, often called "Metro Toronto," is Ontario's largest municipality. Metro Toronto is similar to a regional municipality. If you live in the City of Toronto, the City of Scarborough, the City of North York, the City of Etobicoke, the City of York or the Borough of East York, you live in Metropolitan Toronto.

Improvement Districts

In many areas of Northern Ontario there are not enough people to require municipal government. If an industry begins operating in such an area, arrangements must be made to provide services for the people who will be living there. To provide these services quickly, the province may establish an improvement district. An improvement district is a municipality that is managed by trustees appointed by the Ontario Government. Once the community becomes established, the improvement district will be replaced by a township with an elected municipal council.

Municipal Councils

A municipality is governed by the municipal council. Council's job is to make decisions about municipal services, and to use the money it collects from its taxpayers as wisely as possible. The members of council, called councillors or aldermen, are elected by the municipality's voters. Council members are paid by the municipality for their services. In smaller municipalities, members of council usually serve part-time and work at other jobs as well. In large cities the work of council is more complex, councillors are paid more, and many of them devote all their time to municipal concerns.

Councils must make decisions about a long list of municipal services, including:

- fire protection
- building and maintaining roads and sidewalks
- public transit, such as buses
- street lighting
- water and sewer services
- street cleaning and snow plowing
- planning new housing and business developments
- building and maintaining parks and arenas
- controlling animals
- collecting and disposing of garbage
- operating libraries, daycare centres for small children and homes for the aged

Because of the large number of services they provide, many municipalities divide their council into committees. Each committee studies certain services and makes recommendations to the entire council concerning them. For example, a public works committee might look after road construction and maintenance, storm sewers, street lighting, tree planting and removal, traffic problems and public transit.

Meetings of council or of council committees are held on a regular basis, normally once or twice a month. Council meetings are open to the public, and residents are encouraged to attend. To find out the dates and times of meetings in your municipality, telephone the municipality. The phone number is in the blue pages at the back of the telephone directory under "Municipalities."

How Does Council Govern?

At council meetings the members discuss and act on matters of importance to the municipality. Usually matters come before council in three basic ways:

- members of council bring issues that concern them to council's attention;
- the staff of the municipality identify problems and ask council to consider them;
- individuals, businesses or institutions can ask council to consider a matter that affects them.

All of these items are placed on the council meeting agenda (the list of items to be discussed at the council meeting). When council decides that it needs more information on an issue, it asks the municipal staff to conduct any necessary research and to prepare a report. The issue may also be studied by a council committee. When council has all the information it requires, it will discuss the matter and decide what to do.

If council decides that action is necessary it will probably pass a by-law. By-laws are laws that are in effect only within the boundaries of the municipality. While a municipality may pass by-laws on many matters, the provincial government places limits on the actions a municipality may take. A municipality may pass by-laws only on matters that the province has given it authority to do so.

Bringing a Matter to Council's Attention

One of the advantages of local government is the ease with which you can participate in the decision-making process. As a resident, you have the right to express your opinion on local government issues. You may do this by calling your municipal councillors, or by writing to the council, in care of the municipal clerk. You may also ask to speak at a council or council committee meeting. Once again, you should make such a request through the municipal clerk's office.

LOCAL BOARDS AND COMMISSIONS

Many municipalities establish boards and commissions to advise council on various services such as libraries, housing and recreation facilities. Council appoints people from the community to serve on these boards. If you are interested in serving on a particular board, contact the municipal clerk. The clerk can tell you when council will next be making appointments to the board. You can also watch for advertisements in the local newspaper for volunteers to serve on a board or commission.

BOARDS OF EDUCATION

Boards of education, often called school boards, are an important part of local government. The Ontario Government, through the Ministry of Education, establishes the general policy for schools throughout the province. Locally, school boards elected by the residents decide how best to meet the needs of their students, within the guidelines set by the province. Board members, called "trustees," administer the building and maintenance of schools, hire the teachers and other staff needed to run them, authorize educational programs and approve the textbooks to be used.

If you have a concern about education in your area, call or write to your trustees or to your board of education, care of the board's director of education.

PUBLIC UTILITIES COMMISSIONS

In many communities, a public utilities commission supplies electricity. The commission's responsibilities include:

- setting the prices local residents and businesses pay for electricity;
- planning the provision of electricity to new commercial, industrial and residential developments;
- management of the electric utility.

The public utilities commission may also be responsible for other services such as water purification and distribution, and public transit. In places where it only supplies electric service, the commission may be known as the hydro-electric commission.

Public utilities commissions may be appointed by municipal councils or elected by the residents. Where there is no commission, electricity is provided by the municipality.

LOCAL GOVERNMENT ELECTIONS

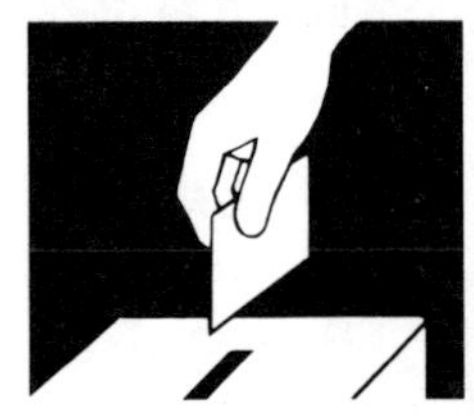

Members of local municipal councils, school boards and some public utilities commissions are elected by the people they serve.

How Are Municipal Councillors Elected?

The way councillors are elected differs from municipality to municipality. There are two methods of electing municipal councillors:

- at large
- by ward

In a municipality where the councillors are elected at large, all councillors represent the entire municipality. In an election, the voters choose among all candidates who are running in the election. If eight councillors are to be elected to municipal council, for example, each voter may vote for eight candidates. When the votes are counted, the eight candidates with the highest number of votes win the election and become the new councillors.

Many larger municipalities are divided into geographic areas called wards. Depending on the municipality, each ward may have one, two or even three representatives on council. Voters in each ward can choose only among the candidates who are running for election in that ward. For example, if a municipality has eight council members and four wards, two councillors will be elected from each ward. Each voter chooses two candidates from among the candidates running in that ward. In each ward, the two candidates with the highest number of votes will serve on council.

What About Metro Toronto Council?

Metro Toronto councillors are elected directly to Metro Council by voters in each ward. Metro Council also includes the mayors of the six local municipalities which form Metro Toronto. One of the members of council is chosen by the council itself to be Metro chairman.

How Is The Head of Council Elected?

The head of a local council is always elected at large by all of the voters in the municipality. In a city or town, the head of council is called a mayor. In a village or township, the head of council is called a reeve. A deputy reeve is also elected in some municipalities.

What about County Councils?

Members of county council are not elected directly by the voters. Instead, reeves and some deputy reeves from the local councils also sit on county councils.

The head of county council is called a warden. The council itself selects the warden each year from among its members.

What about Regional Councils?

Regional council members are selected in various ways. Some are elected by the voters to sit on regional council. Some are elected to sit on both the regional council and the local municipal council. In some municipalities, members of local municipal councils are appointed by their councils to serve at the regional level. The mayor or reeve of a local municipality is always a member of the regional council.

The head of a regional council is called a chairman. The chairman is chosen by the members of council. An exception is the Region of Hamilton-Wentworth, where the chairman is elected by the voters at large.

How Are School Boards Elected?

In Ontario, there are two publicly supported school systems, a "public" school system, and a Roman Catholic "separate" school system. Each system has its own local boards in most areas.

School trustees for both public and separate school boards are elected at the same time as municipal councillors. If you are Roman Catholic, you may vote for public school trustees or separate school trustees, but not both. To vote for separate school trustees, you must assign the school support part of your property taxes to the separate school board. Unless you request that your taxes are paid to the separate school board, they will automatically go to the public school board.

In many areas of the province, education is available in both of Canada's official languages – English and French. School boards in these areas have English and French language sections to administer the two language programs. If your school board has English and French language sections, you may vote for either English or French language trustees. You cannot vote for both.

How Are Public Utilities Commissions Elected?

Where the public utilities commission is elected, it consists of:

- the head of the local municipal council; and
- two or four elected commissioners.

Commission members are elected at the same time as municipal councillors and school board trustees.

When Are Local Elections Held?

Local elections in Ontario are held every three years on the second Monday in November. For example, 1988, 1991 and 1994 are municipal election years.

Who Can Vote in the Elections?

Anyone can vote in a municipal election who, on the day of the election, is:

- 18 years of age or older;
- a Canadian citizen; and
- either a resident of the municipality or a property owner or tenant in the municipality during a specified period just before the election.

To be able to vote, your name must be on the list of eligible voters, called a polling list.

If you are on the polling list, you should receive a card in the mail telling you that you are eligible to vote. If you think you are eligible to vote, but have not received a card by mid-September in an election year, call your municipal clerk. The clerk will tell you what to do in order to be able to vote.

Who Can Be a Candidate?

Any person who is eligible to vote may be a candidate for a position on a municipal council or public utilities commission. To be a candidate for a school board, you must meet certain qualifications which apply only to boards of education. For more detailed information, contact the director of education for your board.

Each candidate must file a nomination paper with the municipal clerk at least twenty-one days before polling day. The nomination paper must be signed by at least ten other qualified voters.

When people speak about candidates in federal or provincial elections, they usually refer to the political party that each candidate represents. In municipal elections, although people may know which political party a candidate supports, the candidates are not elected to represent a political party.

Where to Vote

The place where people vote is called a poll, or polling place. Each poll has one or more voting compartments, so that voters can mark their votes in secrecy.

Typical locations for polling places are schools, community centres, churches and apartment buildings. Wherever possible, polling places are made accessible to persons with physical handicaps.

If you are eligible to vote, you should receive a card telling you where your polling place is. If you do not receive a card, or if you have any questions about where to vote, call the municipal clerk.

Who Runs the Election?

A local election is the responsibility of the municipal clerk, who serves as the returning officer. The returning officer hires, trains and pays the poll officials and makes sure that the election is conducted fairly.

Each polling place is looked after by a deputy returning officer and a poll clerk. They supervise the vote. If you have any questions, they will be able to help you.

When Are the Election Results Known?

The returning officer must announce the results of all local elections three days after the election at the latest.

However, results are usually known on election night and are reported on television and radio. By the next day more detailed reports appear in newspapers.

LOCAL GOVERNMENT FUNDING

Local governments in Ontario spend about $18 billion each year. Half of this amount is for education.

About one-third of the $18 billion comes from property taxes. Less than one-third comes from transit fares, rentals at the municipal arena, charges for parking and other "user fees." The balance comes from grants and subsidies from the Ontario Government and the Federal Government.

The people and businesses that use electricity pay for what they use. Your tax dollars are not used to support electric services.

Property Taxes

Your local government must collect property taxes from each property owner. Municipal and school board taxes are collected by the local municipality on the same tax bill. Tenants pay a portion of their landlord's taxes through their rent.

How does the municipality know how much tax each property owner should pay? There are three steps in setting the amount.

1) Assessing the Property

Assessing the value of property is the responsibility of the provincial government. Each property is examined by an "assessor," a person skilled at determining the value of property. The assessor assigns a value to the property based on the amount the property would be worth if it was sold. The assessed value, called the property assessment, is not the actual dollar value of the property, but only a percentage of it.

If you wish to know the assessed value of any property, visit the municipal clerk's office and ask to see the assessment roll. The assessed value of each property in your municipality is listed on the roll. If the assessed value of your property changes, you will receive a Notice of Assessment, telling you what the new assessment is. A sample of a Notice of Assessment is on the following page.

Notice of Property Valuation (Notice of Assessment)

① Effective From	Property Identifier (Roll Number)	Neighbourhood
	24 01 020 260 069 25 0000	205
C4	Municipality: Your Municipality	

This Notice of Property Valuation shows the **Assessed Value of the property** which you own or occupy. This assessment is the value on which property taxes (municipal and education) will be levied based on mill rates calculated by your municipality. Mill rates are established to raise the funds to meet municipal, county or region and school board needs.

The relationship between assessment and tax is: **Assessed Value X Mill Rate = Taxes.**

Additional information about the numbered items can be found on the reverse side.

Name and Address of Person(s) Assessed

OWNER **Your Name**

Your Address

② School Support Designation: PUBLIC

Location and Description of Property: PLAN M253 LOT 8

Frontage	Depth	Area
61.48	115.42	

③ For the purpose of Assessment, this property is classed as	④ Estimated Market Value in 1984	X	⑤ Property Class %	=	Assessed Value	⑥ Type of Mill Rate to be used for Taxation	⑦ Business Assessment
RESIDENTIAL	181,000		7.200%		13,032	RESIDENTIAL	NOT APPLICABLE

ALL PROPERTIES IN YOUR MUNICIPALITY HAVE BEEN REASSESSED THIS YEAR.

SAMPLE

If you require any assistance, please contact the Regional Assessment Office at

Your Regional Office

You may meet with an accessor to discuss any of the information shown on this Notice at the Open House Session(s) listed below.

An amended Notice will be issued if a correction should be made to any information shown on this Notice before

Notice of Complaint under section 39 of the Assessment Act (Appeal) If you believe you have been improperly assessed, you or your agent may lodge a complaint by completing the reverse side and forwarding to

Regional Registrar, Assessment Review Board
SUITE 300
390 DAVIS DR
NEWMARKET ONT L3Y 2N9

Mail Complaint by

Important:
If your previous assessment is under appeal at the time you receive this Notice, or if this Notice does not reflect the most recent decision of the Board, it is necessary that you again lodge a complaint with the Assessment Review Board against this assessment.

Property Identifier (Roll Number)	Neighbourhood
24 01 020 260 069 25 0000	205

2091A (8609)

If you feel your property has been unfairly assessed, you can do a number of things. First, talk with a provincial assessor at the regional assessment office. The address and telephone number of your regional office is listed on the Notice of Assessment form. You may call your regional office at any time for assistance or for an explanation of your assessment.

Open houses are held shortly after notices of changes in assessment are sent out. Open houses are informal get-togethers usually held at local schools or halls to allow owners who have questions about their assessment to discuss them with the assessors. If you cannot attend an open house, you can make an appointment to meet the assessor elsewhere.

If, after talking to an assessor, you are not satisfied, you may appeal your assessment to the Assessment Review Board. The board may lower your assessment if it feels that a decrease is justified. Your property assessor will help you in making the appeal and will explain the appeal procedures to you.

2) Setting the Mill Rate

The property tax you pay is based on your property assessment and the mill rate.

The mill rate is set by the municipality each year:

- First, council calculates how much it will cost to provide the needed municipal services.
- Next, council estimates the amount of revenue that the provincial government will supply through grants. To that total it adds the amount it expects to raise through user fees. This amount is subtracted from the total cost of services as calculated above.
- Council establishes a mill rate that will allow the remaining amount to be collected from the property owners.

The mill rate is a number based on each $1,000 of property assessment. For example, a mill rate of 60 means that your local government is going to charge $60 in taxes on each $1,000 of assessment.

3) Calculating Your Taxes

Once the assessment and the mill rate are set, the municipality calculates each property owner's taxes by:

- dividing the assessed value of the property by 1,000, and
- multiplying the result by the mill rate.

For example, if the assessed value of your property is $6,000 and the mill rate is 60, your municipal taxes would be $360.

Paying Your Property Taxes

If you own property, a property tax bill showing the amount of property taxes you must pay and when payment is due, will be sent to you.

"Interim" Tax Bill

Local government tax rates are often not finalized until several months into each new year. Yet municipalities and schools still have to spend money during these months. Therefore for the first part of the year, most municipalities send out "interim" tax bills. These are based on the previous year's taxes. Once the tax rates are finalized, any necessary adjustments to your taxes will be made on the bill for the remainder of the year.

Instalments

Municipalities often arrange for taxes to be paid in instalments. This gives the municipality a continuing flow of money to pay its bills, and it allows you to make a series of smaller payments rather than paying the entire amount at once.

The person whose name appears on the tax bill is responsible for paying the property taxes. In most municipalities, taxes may be paid at the municipal office or at any chartered bank or trust company listed on the tax bill. If you want to know more about your taxes, contact your municipal treasurer. Samples of an Interim Tax Bill and a Regular Realty Tax Bill are on the following page.

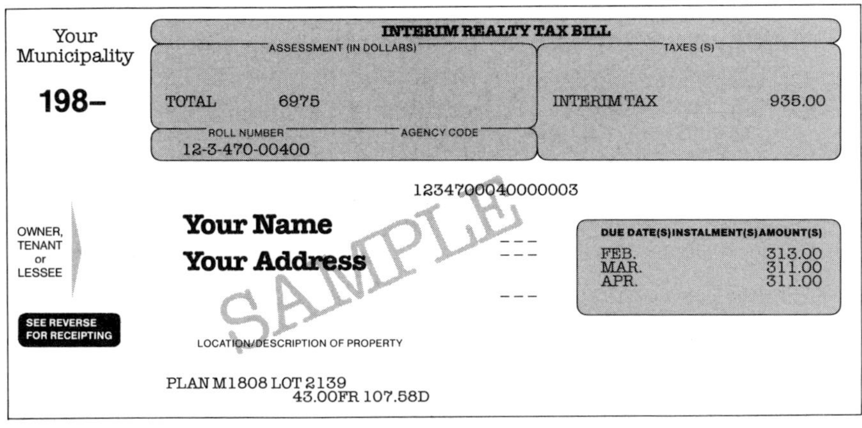

Your Municipality

198–

INTERIM REALTY TAX BILL

ASSESSMENT (IN DOLLARS)

TOTAL 6975

TAXES (S)

INTERIM TAX 935.00

ROLL NUMBER 12-3-470-00400

AGENCY CODE

1234700040000003

OWNER, TENANT or LESSEE

Your Name
Your Address

SAMPLE

DUE DATE(S)	INSTALMENT(S)	AMOUNT(S)
FEB.		313.00
MAR.		311.00
APR.		311.00

SEE REVERSE FOR RECEIPTING

LOCATION/DESCRIPTION OF PROPERTY

PLAN M1808 LOT 2139
43.00FR 107.58D

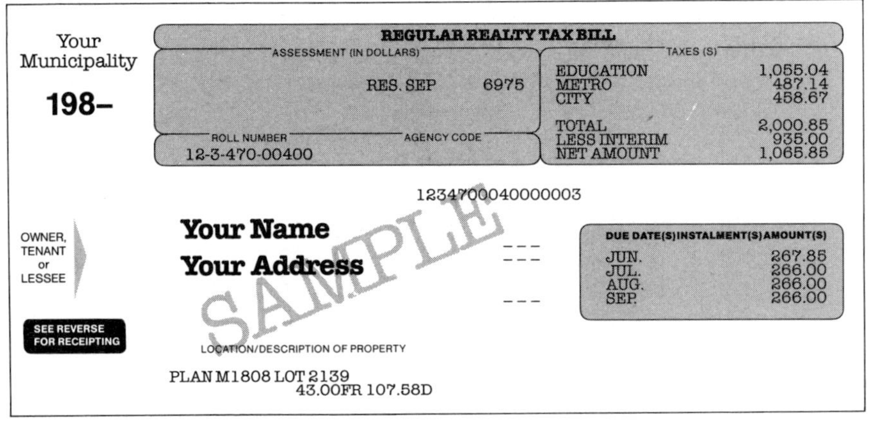

Your Municipality

198–

REGULAR REALTY TAX BILL

ASSESSMENT (IN DOLLARS)

RES. SEP 6975

TAXES (S)

EDUCATION	1,055.04
METRO	487.14
CITY	458.67
TOTAL	2,000.85
LESS INTERIM	935.00
NET AMOUNT	1,065.85

ROLL NUMBER 12-3-470-00400

AGENCY CODE

1234700040000003

OWNER, TENANT or LESSEE

Your Name
Your Address

SAMPLE

DUE DATE(S)	INSTALMENT(S)	AMOUNT(S)
JUN.		267.85
JUL.		266.00
AUG.		266.00
SEP.		266.00

SEE REVERSE FOR RECEIPTING

LOCATION/DESCRIPTION OF PROPERTY

PLAN M1808 LOT 2139
43.00FR 107.58D

What Happens if Taxes Are Not Paid?

Taxes should be paid on or before the due date indicated on the tax bill. Municipalities charge interest on taxes that are not paid on time. If taxes remain unpaid at the end of the year, the municipality may require that a penalty be paid in addition to the taxes and any interest owing.

If taxes remain unpaid for three years, the municipality may sell the property for non-payment of property taxes. Land which has not yet been built on may be sold for non-payment after two years.

Tax Grants for Senior Citizens

Ontario residents who are over sixty-five years of age are entitled to receive a Property Tax Grant from the Ontario government. The Property Tax Grant provides up to $600 per household to offset municipal and school taxes paid by homeowners. Tenants who are senior citizens qualify for $600 or 20% of the rent on a principal residence whichever is lower.

Most people who receive Old Age Security (OAS) and other seniors who previously received a Property Tax Grant will automatically receive application forms in late August. Other seniors should contact the Ontario Ministry of Revenue, Taxpayer Services Branch:

- in Metro Toronto dial 965-8470
- in Oshawa dial 433-5155
- in area code 807, dial 1-800-263-3792
- in area code 416, dial 1-800-263-7700
- in area code 519, 613 and 705, dial 1-800-263-3960

GUIDE TO LOCAL GOVERNMENT SERVICES

The rest of this handbook is a guide to the services local government provides. Because of differences in type and size, not all municipalities provide the same services. In general, the large, urban municipalities offer more services to their residents than do the small, rural municipalities. This guidebook describes the services offered in most urban municipalities. If, after reading this guide, you have any questions about the services provided in your own municipality, contact your municipal office. The number is in the Municipal Government section of the blue pages, at the back of your telephone directory.

To find information on a service quickly, refer to the table of contents at the front of this book.

THE MUNICIPAL CLERK'S OFFICE

There is a municipal clerk in every municipality. It is part of the clerk's job to know which municipal departments or employees do what and where they can be reached. So if you need municipal assistance or information but do not know who to talk to, call the municipal clerk. The clerk's office can be found in the municipal building or offices.

In addition to being a key source of information, the clerk's office handles many other duties, which usually include:

- issuing marriage licences
- recording births, deaths and marriages
- organizing local government elections
- notifying residents of public meetings
- selling dog licences

The municipal clerk is also in charge of keeping all municipal documents. To get a copy of a by-law, report or other document, visit the clerk's office.

Business Licences

A special licence is required to carry on many different businesses or trades in a municipality. If you want to open a restaurant, start a taxicab company or operate a public parking lot, you will probably need a municipal licence. If you are thinking of starting your own business, call the municipal clerk and ask if you need a licence.

If the answer is yes, the clerk will tell you how to apply for a licence. Your application will describe the business and where you plan to operate it. The clerk will ask other municipal staff, such as fire and building officials, to comment on the application. Then the application, with their comments, goes to council for approval or rejection.

In some municipalities, council appoints a committee or commission to grant licences. If so, the clerk's office will be able to tell you how to apply.

A licence may be taken away if there are numerous complaints about the operation of a business.

POLICE PROTECTION

The task of protecting people and their property is shared by the federal, provincial and local governments.

The federal police force is the Royal Canadian Mounted Police (RCMP). It enforces certain federal laws.

The Ontario Provincial Police (OPP) conducts certain criminal investigations and patrols provincial highways and waterways. The OPP also provides police services in municipalities which do not have a local police force.

Large municipalities generally operate their own police force. In most regional municipalities, a single force provides police protection for all of the municipalities in the region. Metropolitan Toronto also operates one force for all its local municipalities.

The main duties of municipal police forces are to protect people and their property, to catch offenders and to maintain order in the community. In larger municipalities, the police force may also operate youth bureaus and community service bureaus which offer crime prevention and other educational programs.

If You Need Help

The telephone number for the police is listed in the front of your telephone directory. Keep the number close to the phone at all times. If you need police assistance, call and give your name, where you are and the reason you need help.

FIRE PROTECTION

Each municipality decides how it will provide fire protection services. Most large municipalities have full-time fire-fighters. Many smaller municipalities depend on volunteer firefighters.

If a fire breaks out in your home, and you cannot quickly put it out, leave the building immediately. Call the fire department from the nearest available phone. Give the location of the fire. Seconds can mean the difference between success and failure in controlling the fire. The nearest fire station will send firefighters and equipment to fight the fire.

Fire departments may also provide other services, such as fire prevention education and inspection services, performing rescue work, and resuscitating accident and heart attack victims.

AMBULANCE SERVICES

Municipally run ambulance services are available in many larger municipalities. The cost of an ambulance is partially covered by the Ontario Health Insurance Plan (OHIP) if it is medically necessary. Check the front of your telephone directory to see what ambulance services are available in your area. If someone needs emergency medical attention and should not be moved without skilled help or cannot be taken to a hospital by any other means, call the ambulance service.

DIAL 911

In some areas of the province, you can reach the fire department, police and ambulance services by simply dialing 911 on your telephone. Look in the pages at the front of your telephone directory to see if this service is available in your municipality.

TRANSPORTATION SERVICES

Public Transportation

Public transportation in Ontario includes service by train, subway, streetcar, bus and, in some areas, air. Bus service, which is the most common form of public transportation, is provided in most urban areas.

To travel within a municipality, you must have tickets, a pass or cash. Some municipalities sell tickets on the buses. In others, tickets can only be purchased at stations and some stores. Without a ticket or pass you must usually give the driver the exact amount of the fare; the driver will not give you any change back. Senior citizens, children under a certain age, and students with student cards may travel for a lower fare in many municipalities.

Within a municipality, there is normally a set fare per trip, no matter how far you go. If you have to change from one vehicle to another to reach your destination, get a transfer when you pay your fare. You can then continue on to your destination without paying again.

If you are travelling between municipalities, the fare will usually increase according to the distance you are travelling.

Metro Toronto

In Metro Toronto you will find streetcars and a subway system in addition to buses. You can buy tokens as well as tickets and monthly passes. Tickets and tokens can only be purchased at stations and some stores. Paying by cash costs more per trip than buying tickets, tokens or passes.

Do you know how to reach your destination? Many public transit offices provide maps, called "Ride Guides" that show the routes of their buses and other vehicles. You can also phone the public transit office for advice.

Services for the Handicapped

In many municipalities, a special transportation service is available to people who have a physical handicap. If you require such a service, contact the local transit office.

GO Transit

GO (Government of Ontario) transit is a bus and rail service operated by the Ontario Government. It carries passengers between many of the municipalities in and around Metropolitan Toronto. In several municipalities, municipal bus service is free when riding to or from a GO transit station. For more information, contact the nearest GO Transit office or the municipal transit office.

PARKING

Many municipalities restrict parking on some streets. If you park your car where there is a "no parking" sign you may receive a fine, or have your vehicle towed away. Many municipalities also have by-laws which say that vehicles may not be parked on residential streets overnight. To find out if your municipality has such a by-law, contact the municipality.

Where there is a shortage of parking, residents can sometimes apply to the municipality for a permit to park on residential streets overnight. Contact your municipal office to find out about parking in your neighbourhood.

Meter Parking

In commercial areas and on main streets you may find parking meters. When you park by a meter, put enough coins in it to cover the time your vehicle will be in the parking space. This is shown on the meter, usually close to where the money is deposited. If you do not, or the meter shows your time has expired, you may be fined. Check on the meter for the length of time that you are allowed to park; most meters will let you stay one or two hours, but in busy places they may let you stay only 15 minutes. Check also on the hours that meter parking applies; usually you do not have to pay in the evenings or on Sundays.

Parking Fines

If you get a parking ticket, it will require you to pay a fine. Fines may be paid by mail at the address shown on the back of the ticket or sometimes at a chartered bank or trust company. You can either pay the fine or, if you feel that you have been unfairly charged, request a trial.

If you have an unpaid parking fine you will not be able to get your vehicle licence renewed until the fine is paid.

Parking Permits for the Handicapped

Some municipalities provide special stickers for vehicles operated by handicapped persons or by drivers transporting handicapped persons. A vehicle bearing such a sticker is allowed to park in parking spaces reserved for the handicapped. Licence plates bearing the handicapped symbol are issued by the Government of Ontario and can be used in place of the permit.

If you need such a sticker, contact the municipality for information.

ROAD AND SIDEWALK MAINTENANCE

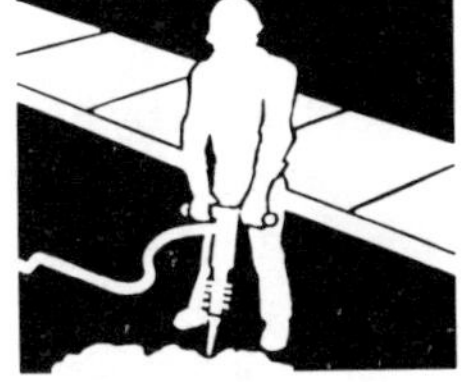

The municipality maintains municipal roads and sidewalks. Maintenance includes cleaning, filling cracks and potholes and doing reconstruction. If you notice an area of road or sidewalk badly in need of repair, contact the municipal public works department or the municipal clerk.

SNOW REMOVAL

Snow removal from public streets is carried out by the municipality. Responsibility for snow removal from municipal sidewalks varies from municipality to municipality. Some municipalities have small plows that clear the sidewalks. Others require owners or tenants to clear the sidewalk in front of their property. If you are not sure whether you must clear the sidewalk, ask your neighbor or contact the municipality.

Some municipalities have special services for senior citizens and for persons with handicaps who are unable to shovel snow themselves. If you need assistance, call the municipality to see if such a service is offered.

STREET LIGHTING

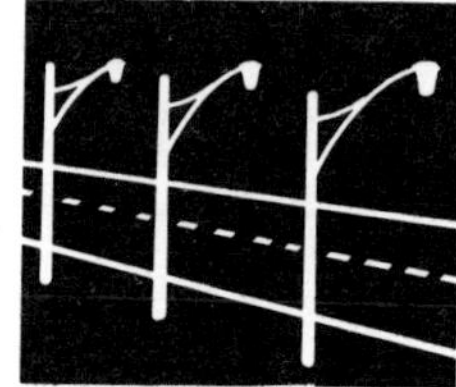

Street lights are installed and maintained by the local municipality or public utilities commission. They should turn on automatically at dusk and off at dawn. If you feel your neighbourhood requires more street lighting or if you wish to report a broken or burned out light, contact the municipal public works department or the public utilities commission.

GARBAGE COLLECTION AND DISPOSAL

Garbage Collection

Garbage collection is a municipal responsibility. In most urban areas, garbage is collected once a week. Most municipalities ask you to follow rules like these:

- Place garbage as close as possible to the curb, without blocking the public sidewalk.
- Put garbage in cans or plastic bags, not cartons or boxes.
- Do not put garbage out before six p.m. on the day before garbage is collected. Remove garbage cans from the street as soon as possible after collection.
- Wrap broken glass in newspaper and then put it in a plastic bag.
- Put leaves and garden refuse in containers. Do not leave them loose by the roadway. Some municipalities have a special collection of leaves each fall.
- Do not put paints and chemicals in with other garbage. Some municipalities have a special collection for these items. Call the municipal public works department for more information.
- Many municipalities have a special spring and fall collection where there is no limit on the size and weight of items to be picked up. Put out items such as large appliances and furniture for collection at that time.
- There is often a special collection of Christmas trees shortly after Christmas.

Recycling

Many municipalities encourage residents to separate materials such as glass bottles and jars, metal cans and newspapers, from the garbage. These items will be picked up separately for recycling. If the municipality recycles these materials, it will need to dispose of less garbage and thus save money.

Burning Garbage

Generally, burning garbage is not permitted. For information about the burning of garbage, contact your municipal fire department.

Where to Get More Information

To inquire about collection times or for more information on recycling, contact your municipal clerk's office or the public works department.

RECREATION AND CULTURE

Residents in most municipalities can enjoy a variety of programs and special events in parks, community recreation centres, ice rinks and schools.

Many municipalities offer a variety of sports programs as well as leisure activities such as painting, pottery, quilting and fitness programs. Recreation centres offer dances and weekly games that give people an opportunity to get together. Many programs are free. Some charge a small fee.

Community centres often need volunteers to help with the activities. If you would like to get involved, or for more information concerning municipal recreation programs, contact your local municipal recreation department.

Parks

Most communities have small neighbourhood parks. These parks usually have a grass playing area and play equipment for children.

Many municipalities also have larger community parks that have picnic areas, nature trails and large open spaces.

Libraries

Many municipalities have a library where people can borrow books for a limited time (usually two or three weeks). Some libraries also lend films, records and cassettes, and have materials in languages other than English. Many libraries also take part in inter-library loan arrangements. This means that once you become a member of one library, you can borrow materials from other libraries in the same region. Most libraries also have a reference section of encyclopedias, dictionaries and other materials that you may use only in the library.

To become a library member, visit the local library and ask for a library card. You may be required to show some identification. There is no charge for the card or to take out library materials. For more information, call your public library. It is listed in the white pages of the telephone book under "Public Library" or under the name of your municipality.

SOCIAL SERVICES

Local governments provide a wide range of programs and services to aid those in need.

General Welfare Assistance

An individual may be eligible for temporary financial assistance if he or she:

- is unemployed and looking for work;
- is unable to work due to short-term illness or long-term disability;
- is a single parent;
- is elderly;
- is a foster child;
- is attending elementary or secondary school with no other means of support.

A person may receive other types of assistance and/or income and still be eligible for General Welfare Assistance (GWA).

The amount of assistance depends on the recipient's income, expenses, family size and the ages of any children. General Welfare Assistance provides money for basic living costs, including food, clothing, shelter and other expenses, such as food required for a medical diet, if needed.

Everyone who qualifies for GWA also receive a comprehensive drug benefit plan and full coverage of their Ontario Hospital Insurance Plan (OHIP) premiums.

Special Assistance and Supplementary Aid

The Special Assistance program provides certain items, services and payments to individuals on low or fixed incomes who require extra financial aid. Applicants may already be receiving other types of assistance, such as Workers' Compensation or Unemployment Insurance. However, applicants do not have to be receiving any type of assistance to qualify for Special Assistance. A fully employed person can be eligible.

Supplementary Aid is provided to recipients of Family Benefits, Old Age Security, Vocational Rehabilitation Service Allowances, GAINS (Guaranteed Annual Income Supplement) Allowances and/or Canada Pension payments to cover special needs, usually on a one-time basis. Benefits are granted to individuals when their budgetary needs, as determined by legislation, exceed their income.

Municipalities may provide Supplementary Aid or Special Assistance for:

- moving or necessary transportation expenses;
- comfort allowances for those in nursing homes (to pay for personal items, candy, newspapers, etc.)
- surgical supplies and prosthetic appliances;
- dental or optical services, including eyeglasses;
- vocational training;
- funerals and burials.

Other Financial and Employment Assistance

Many municipalities offer other services in addition to these financial programs. Services that may be available in your municipality include:

- counselling in matters relating to spousal or child support, including the maintenance and enforcement of court orders;
- assisting with home management, including child care, shopping, meal planning and preparation and money management;
- assisting employable persons to get jobs by providing them with vocational counselling, job searching skills, information on training and job opportunities and child care support;
- providing special services to show unemployed youths how to use available community services and to help them find jobs;
- providing home nursing services to people in need of them through an organization such as the Victorian Order of Nurses;
- paying for or helping to pay for visiting homemakers to enable those who are elderly, disabled, ill or recovering from illness to remain in their own homes and to prevent serious family disruption.

To find out if these services are offered in your municipality, check with your municipal social services office.

Child Care

If you leave your children at home, you must provide a babysitter. If this is not possible, leave your children with a responsible friend or neighbour. In an emergency, local daycare programs may be able to help you.

If you are a single parent or both parents work, you may need a daycare centre or private home daycare for your children. For information about daycare centres, contact the municipality or the local community information centre.

If you are unable to pay the full daycare fee, you may be eligible for help with daycare costs from the local social services department. Subsidized daycare spaces are limited, and there may be a waiting list. No subsidies are given for babysitters. For more information about daycare subsidies, contact your municipal social services department.

Children's Aid Societies

Children's aid societies have two main responsibilities. They look after children in need of protection and support families in their child-raising responsibilities. The services of the children's aid society (CAS) in your municipality include:

- programs to prevent family breakups, including parent education and family counselling;
- protection of children from abuse and from situations of distress;
- guidance of mothers-to-be who are on their own;
- foster homes for children needing temporary or long-term placement; and
- adoption services that handle all aspects involved in helping a family arrange for and adjust to an adoption.

Your local children's aid society is listed in the white pages of the phone book.

Services for the Elderly

Municipalities provide services for the elderly. Some of them are listed below.

Aids for Independence

Municipalities often operate services for seniors such as meals-on-wheels, homemakers' and nurses' services and senior volunteers-in-service who help seniors remain at home.

Elderly Persons' Centres

Many municipalities operate elderly persons' centres which offer social, recreational and other activities to encourage seniors to remain active in the community.

Homes For the Aged

Homes for the aged are operated by many municipalities. A range of services is available: some homes are purely residential; others offer extended health care for seniors unable to remain at home. The homes charge a fee for accommodation, meals and services, but medical care is provided by OHIP. A subsidy is provided to those who need it. The needs of applicants are matched with the type of care available by the home. They are admitted on a "first come first served" basis. There may be a waiting period before space is available.

For more information on services for the elderly, contact your municipal clerk or community information centre.

PUBLIC HEALTH SERVICES

Every family should have a family doctor to look after its personal medical needs. Public health units provide general health care in communities throughout Ontario. The Ontario Ministry of Health establishes the type and nature of health care services and municipalities and public health boards are responsible for providing these services.

An important service offered by public health units are the home visits made by public health nurses. They visit aged and handicapped people, parents of newborn infants and ex-psychiatric patients. These nurses also visit schools and teach at pre-natal classes and venereal disease clinics.

Public health inspection is another major function of health units. Health inspectors check food-handling establishments, monitor septic tank installations and are generally responsible for controlling public health risks, including communicable diseases.

Health units' dentistry services teach and encourage preventive dental measures, particularly in the schools. They also provide free dental clinics for those who cannot afford to pay for dental care.

The local health unit may also operate a psychiatric clinic, providing consultation and out-patient treatment to children and adolescents.

For more information about health services, ask your doctor or contact your municipal health unit.

ANIMAL CONTROL

Municipalities are responsible for reducing animal-related health risks and for assisting residents in dealing with nuisance animals. This is done in several ways.

Licensing

In some municipalities, if you own a dog, you must buy a dog licence. Licences are usually sold by the municipal clerk's office or the local Animal Humane Society. You will receive a tag, which you attach to the dog's collar. If the dog is lost, it can be identified by the tag.

Exotic Pets

Some municipalities do not allow people to keep exotic pets within the municipality. (Most pets other than domesticated dogs, cats, birds and rodents are considered exotic.) Urban municipalities often also ban the keeping of farm animals within the municipality. The municipal animal control officer can answer any questions about restrictions on animals. If there is no animal control officer, contact the municipal clerk's office.

Lost Pets

Many municipalities operate a lost and found service to reunite lost pets with their owners. This service may be operated directly by the municipality or through the local Humane Society. If you should lose your dog or cat, call the municipal animal control officer or the Humane Society.

Humane Care

If you have an animal, you must keep it in sanitary condition, and provide it with enough food, water and exercise. If you see an animal being cruelly treated or know of an animal that is being neglected, call the local Humane Society office. The Humane Society will send someone to check on the animal's condition. If the animal is being treated badly, the society may take legal action against the owner.

Animal Bites

If you are bitten by a dog or a wild animal, get immediate medical attention. If possible, have someone keep track of the animal (but stay well away from it). Ask the municipal animal control officer or a humane society representative to come and check the animal for rabies.

LAND USE PLANNING

What is Land Use Planning?

Municipalities in Ontario are growing and changing. They must plan for this growth. If new homes are going to be built, will water and electricity be available? Where will the people do their shopping? Where will the children go to school? Is there a noisy factory nearby that would disturb the residents? Would building the homes destroy a beautiful park or the best land for farming? To deal with questions like these, each municipality sets out an "official plan," which describes how different areas of the municipality are to develop.

The Zoning By-law

To make sure the official plan is followed, municipalities pass "zoning by-laws." A zoning by-law divides the municipality into smaller areas, called zones. The by-law says how the land within each zone can be used (for example, industrial, commercial or residential). It also sets limits on building height, the distance structures must be from the property line, the size the buildings are allowed to be, and other such matters.

How Does the Zoning By-law Affect You?

Any new development that does not meet the municipality's zoning by-law is not permitted. Before you build a house or other structure, make sure that it meets all of the zoning requirements. Also check the zoning requirements if you want to expand an existing building or plan to change a building's use. For example, in many areas, turning a single-family dwelling into a duplex or into commercial office space is not permitted.

If you want to know the zoning for a particular property, contact the municipal planning or building department or, where no such department exists, the municipal clerk.

How Is a Zoning By-law Changed?

Property owners may apply to the municipality to have the zoning for their property changed. This is called a "rezoning." When the municipality receives an application for a rezoning, it must notify the public about the application and hold a public meeting to allow people living nearby to express their views. Notice of the meeting is given in advance, usually through local newspapers or by mail.

If you are concerned about a zoning application that might affect you, you can take part in the decision-making process by:

- finding out as much as possible about the proposed change to the by-law;
- attending the public meeting and expressing your opinions;
- discussing the proposal with municipal staff and council members;
- sending your views in writing to the municipal clerk.

What if You Want Your Own Zoning Changed?

If you want to use or develop your property in a way that is not allowed by the existing zoning by-law, you may have to apply for a rezoning. Before you apply, discuss your proposal with the municipality's planning staff. They can offer advice on how to proceed with a formal application. Most municipalities charge an application fee.

When your application is received, the municipality will notify the affected public and hold a public meeting to discuss it. Council may also consult with planning staff and interested agencies, such as the county or regional government, before making a decision. After considering all concerns and opinions, council will decide whether to pass your proposed rezoning, pass it with changes, or reject it.

What Right of Appeal Do You Have?

If council rejects your proposed zoning change, or if you disagree with council's decision on a change requested by someone else, you can make an appeal to the Ontario Municipal Board (OMB). The OMB is an independent appeal board that hears disputes about planning concerns. If you file an appeal, the OMB will hold a public hearing where you will have an opportunity to present your views. In most cases, the Board's decision is final.

To find out more about the OMB, contact the municipal planning department, or call the OMB's Information Officer at (416) 598-2266, extension 212 or 213.

What If All You Need Is a Minor Change in the By-Law?

If you want to build a structure that does not quite meet the zoning by-law's requirements, you can apply for an exemption to the by-law. This is called a "minor variance." If you receive a minor variance, you do not have to make a formal rezoning application.

To obtain a minor variance, you must apply to the Committee of Adjustment. The committee of adjustment is made up of citizens appointed by the local council to deal with minor problems in meeting by-law standards. The committee will tell you when and where your application will be discussed. They will invite you and any other interested persons to speak at the meeting.

For more information on applying for a minor variance, contact the Secretary-Treasurer for the Committee of Adjustment for your municipality.

Land Severance

You might want to split (sever) your property into two or more pieces, so that you can sell, lease or mortgage part of the property. Because it affects the surrounding property owners and the municipality's ability to provide services, you must obtain approval before dividing the property.

If only a few lots are to be created, this is called land severance. To find out who is responsible for approving a land severance in your area, and how to apply, contact the municipal clerk or planning department.

If you want to divide the property into more than four or five lots, you must submit a special plan of the lots you intend to create, called a "plan of subdivision," to the municipality for approval. Contact your municipal planning department for more information.

BUILDING

Building Permits

If you wish to construct a building or renovate or add to an existing one, you must have a building permit from your municipality. Building permits allow a municipality to regulate the types of construction in the community and to ensure that structures are safe and meet the requirements of the Ontario Building Code.

The Building Code sets standards for materials and design for all building construction and renovations. You must obtain a building permit before you:

- construct a new building or structure on your property;
- make alterations, additions or repairs to a building;
- excavate or construct a foundation;
- install heating, plumbing, an air-conditioning system or fireplace;

- put up a temporary building or mobile home;
- renovate or convert an existing building.

When thinking about any kind of construction, it is a good idea to discuss your plans with municipal building staff first. They can advise you about any other permits or approvals you might need, such as a demolition permit, a minor variance or an electrical permit. If you are not sure whether you need a building permit or not, call a municipal building officer.

How to Apply for a Building Permit

Applications for building permits can be obtained from the municipal building department or building officer. Along with an application, you must submit sketches, drawings, plans and other documents. You may have to pay an application fee and additional charges for such services as property surveys and connection to the municipal water supply. To check the exact requirements of the permit application, contact a building officer.

When you apply for a permit, the municipal building officer will examine your plans to make sure they meet the Ontario Building Code requirements and the municipality's zoning bylaw. If the proposed work meets all of the requirements and the required fees are paid, the municipality must issue the permit to you. If it does not meet all of the requirements, the building officer will tell you the reasons, and will describe any changes that might resolve the problem.

Building Inspections

Building permits often list inspections that must be done during construction. The inspector's job is to make sure that the work is being done according to the building code, your permit and the approved building plans. The inspector must be able to see the part of the construction he or she is to inspect.

If the inspector finds that the work being done differs from the approved plans, you will be advised to correct the situation. If work continues without the problem being fixed, the municipality can take you to court.

When work begins, the permit must be displayed in a window or other place where it can easily be seen by a municipal inspector. You must also keep a copy of the building plan where the work is being done, and tell your local building officer about any changes to the plans as soon as possible.

Changes will require approval in the same way as the original building plans.

Building Demolition

Before you demolish a building or part of a building, you must apply for a demolition permit. The process is similar to that for a building permit. For more information, consult your local building officer.

Property Standards By-laws

Many municipalities have a property standards by-law requiring that, for health and safety reasons, buildings be kept in good repair and that properties be kept clear of debris. If you are a tenant, and are concerned about your building, first contact the building manager about the problem. If the problem is not fixed, contact the municipal clerk to find out whether the municipality has a property standards by-law, and what help the municipality can give you to resolve the problem.

Signs, Awnings, Fences and Hedges

Many municipalities have by-laws setting out requirements for the hanging of awnings or canopies, the size and location of signs and the height and location of fences and hedges. If you are planning to install any of these, first contact the municipal clerk or building department to find out what the requirements are.

When a fence is built along the property line between two pieces of land, the cost of the fence is usually shared by the property owners on either side. If the two owners cannot agree on how the cost should be shared, either owner may ask the municipality to appoint independent arbitrators, called fence-viewers, to divide the costs. This can only be done before the fence is built.

For more information on fence-viewers, contact the municipal clerk.

EDUCATION

Free access to elementary and secondary education is the right of every child or adult in Ontario.

The law requires all children between the ages of six and sixteen to attend school. The school year begins in the first week of September, and ends in the last week of June.

Elementary School

Any child whose sixth birthday is before the first day of school must start grade one in September. Those who turn six after the first day of school, but before a date set by the local school board (usually December 31), may also begin in September, if the parents wish. Elementary school has eight grades.

Senior kindergarten is offered by most school boards. It accepts children who will turn five by the end of December in that year. Some school boards also offer junior kindergarten which accepts children whose fourth birthday comes before the end of the calendar year. For information on kindergarten in your municipality, contact your local board of education.

Secondary School

Secondary School offers a wide variety of courses to prepare students for employment or post-secondary education.

If students over 16 years of age cannot attend school full-time, they may be able to complete their secondary education through part-time school attendance or through correspondence courses. For more information, ask at your local secondary school.

Enrolling Your Child in School

To enrol your child in school, watch for a notice in the local paper about registration day. This is usually in the spring before the child starts school. Your local school board office can also give you the date. If you miss registration day or arrive in Ontario in the middle of a school year, contact your local school board as soon as possible.

To register your child in school, go to your local school. Take with you:

- your child's birth certificate or passport;
- some proof of your child's immigration status (if needed);
- your child's immunization documents.

To register your child in a Roman Catholic separate school, you will also have to provide proof of school support (your tax bill), and a baptismal certificate.

If you need more information about starting school, contact the local school principal or the school board.

School Bus Service

To find out whether there is school bus service in your area, contact the local school principal or the school board.

Language Instruction

Many schools have special programs for children who need to learn English. They may also have heritage language programs outside of normal school hours. These programs allow children to study their native language or other languages of their choice. English and French are official languages and are not included in the heritage language programs.

Special Programs

Other programs, such as French immersion programs, for non-francophone French-speaking students, programs for exceptional children and programs for children with physical or mental handicaps are offered in many areas. To find out what programs are available to children in your area, contact your local school board.

Adult Education

Adult education courses are provided by boards of education, community colleges and universities. These courses are usually offered in the evenings to allow people who work during the day to attend.

For more information, contact the school boards, colleges and universities in your area.

ELECTRICITY

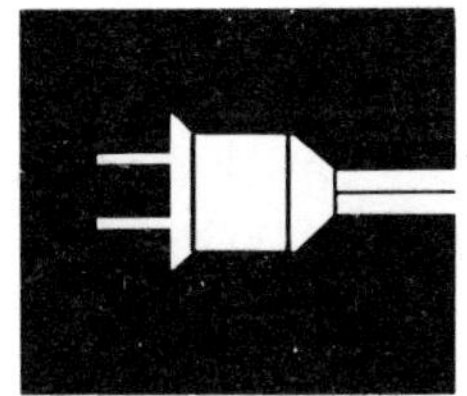

Your Electricity Bill

If you pay for your electricity directly, and not through rent to a landlord, you will receive a bill from the local public utilities commission or municipality. The amount charged is usually for two months and is for the actual amount of electricity used during that time.

Depending on the municipality you live in, your public utilities bill might also include charges for water and/or sewer usage.

Advice on Saving Energy

Every time you use electricity, it costs you money. There are many ways to reduce the amount of electricity you use. Your public utilities commission can give you information on how to use less electricity and save money. Information is also available on how to keep your home warmer in winter and save on your home heating bills.

For more information on electrical services, or on using less energy, call the public utilities commission. It is listed in the white pages of the telephone book under the name of your municipality's Public Utilities Commission, or its Hydro Electric Commission.

WATER AND SEWER SERVICES

The purification and distribution of water and the provision of sewer services are a municipal responsibility. These services are provided mainly in urban areas. In most rural areas, property owners use wells and septic systems at their own expense.

In many places you are charged for the use of water as determined by reading your water meter. You may also pay a "sewer surcharge" for sewer services. The surcharge is based on the amount of water you use. If you live in a home without a meter, you will pay a fixed amount for water and sewer services.

Municipalities collect for water and sewer in several ways. For example, the City of Toronto bills for water separately, twice a year. Because most houses are not metered, the amount is a fixed charge. In the City of Scarborough, the public utilities commission collects for electricity and water. Sewer charges are included on the tax bill in all of the municipalities in Metropolitan Toronto. In the City of Cambridge, the public utilities commission collects for electricity, water and sewer charges. A sample of a Hydro-Electric Commission bill is on the following page.

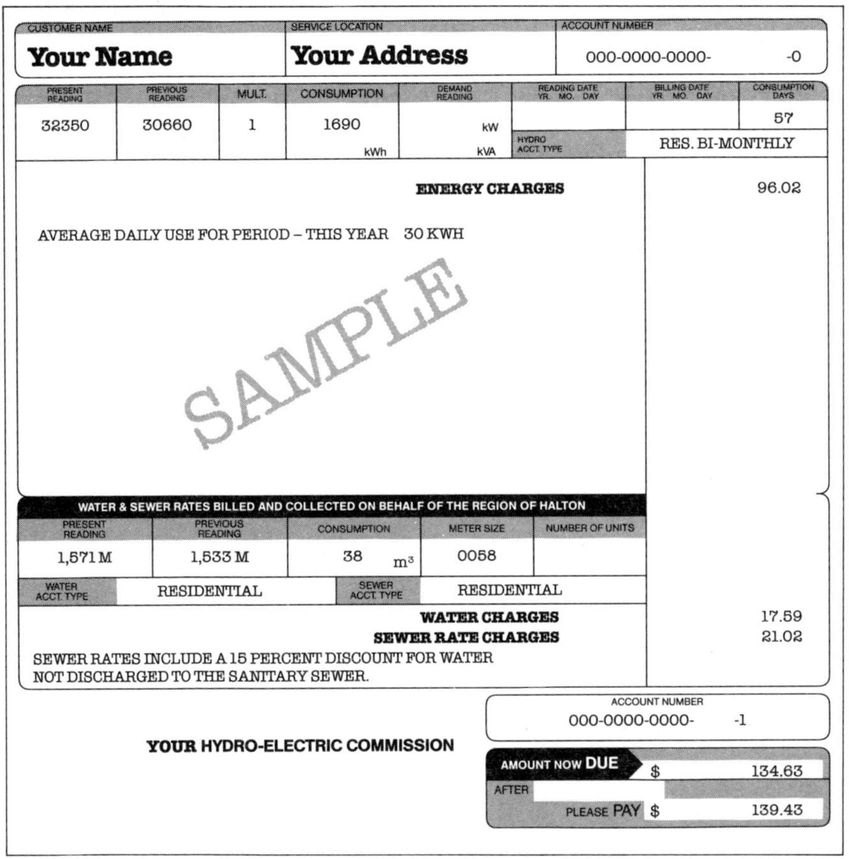

CUSTOMER NAME	SERVICE LOCATION	ACCOUNT NUMBER
Your Name	Your Address	000-0000-0000- -0

PRESENT READING	PREVIOUS READING	MULT.	CONSUMPTION	DEMAND READING	READING DATE YR. MO. DAY	BILLING DATE YR. MO. DAY	CONSUMPTION DAYS
32350	30660	1	1690 kWh	kW kVA			57
					HYDRO ACCT. TYPE	RES. BI-MONTHLY	

ENERGY CHARGES 96.02

AVERAGE DAILY USE FOR PERIOD – THIS YEAR 30 KWH

SAMPLE

WATER & SEWER RATES BILLED AND COLLECTED ON BEHALF OF THE REGION OF HALTON

PRESENT READING	PREVIOUS READING	CONSUMPTION	METER SIZE	NUMBER OF UNITS
1,571 M	1,533 M	38 m^3	0058	

WATER ACCT. TYPE	RESIDENTIAL	SEWER ACCT. TYPE	RESIDENTIAL

WATER CHARGES 17.59
SEWER RATE CHARGES 21.02

SEWER RATES INCLUDE A 15 PERCENT DISCOUNT FOR WATER NOT DISCHARGED TO THE SANITARY SEWER.

ACCOUNT NUMBER 000-0000-0000- -1

YOUR HYDRO-ELECTRIC COMMISSION

AMOUNT NOW DUE $ 134.63
AFTER
PLEASE PAY $ 139.43

Having Your Meter Read

If your meters (hydro and water) are located outside of the house, you must make sure that the way is clear so that the meter can be read. If either meter is inside your home, the meter reader will need to enter. Before letting anyone in to read a meter, ask to see proper identification. If you do not wish the meter reader to enter, or if you are not at home, a card will be left for you to fill in and mail. In some municipalities, you may also provide the required information by phone.

WHERE TO FIND OUT MORE

If you want more information on any municipal service or on how to participate in local government, call your municipality. The telephone number is in the blue pages at the back of the telephone directory. If you have a question about a particular service, call the department which provides that service. If you do not know whom to call, contact the municipal clerk. He or she will be able to answer your question, or tell you where to call.

Many municipalities publish a municipal directory giving information on the municipality and its services. In some of the larger municipalities, the directory is available in several languages. Ask the municipal clerk if a directory is available in your municipality.

GLOSSARY

Alderman: See "councillor."

Assessment Roll: A record of the assessed value of each property in a municipality.

At Large Election: An election system in which all elected candidates represent the entire municipality.

Board of Education: See "school board."

Building Permit: Formal, written permission to begin construction of or renovations to a building.

By-Laws: Laws passed by a municipality that are in effect only within the boundaries of the municipality.

Chairman of Regional Council: The head of a regional municipal council usually chosen by the members of council.

City: A municipality with a large population. A city located in a county does not pay for, or receive, services offered by the county.

Committee of Adjustment: A committee of citizens appointed by the local council to deal with requests for minor exemptions or "variances" from municipal by-law standards.

Councillors: Members of municipal council elected to represent the interests of the citizens. Councillors may be elected at large or by ward. Councillors are sometimes called aldermen.

County: An upper level of municipal government used mainly in rural areas. Counties provide services which cannot be provided as efficiently by individual local municipalities. The lower level of municipal government includes townships, villages and towns within the county.

General Welfare Assistance: An income support program providing financial assistance to people who are otherwise without support.

Hydro-Electric Commission: A Public Utilities Commission that oversees only the provision of electrical services.

Improvement District: A municipality in Northern Ontario which is managed by provincially-appointed trustees. An improvement district is established in unsettled or sparsely settled areas where a new industry is located and municipal government is needed immediately. The improvement district is replaced by a township when the community becomes established.

Interim Tax Bill: A bill requiring payment of taxes for the first part of the year based on the previous year's taxes.

Land Severance: Dividing land into smaller sections by the property owner for the purpose of selling, leasing or mortgaging.

Land Use Planning: Managing the development and use of land using such tools as official plans and zoning by-laws. Planning ensures that as a municipality grows, necessary services such as streets and schools are not over-burdened and essential elements of the natural environment are preserved.

Local Boards: Appointed bodies that oversee various operations of a municipality. For example, library boards, local boards of health.

Mayor: The head of council in a city or town, elected at large.

Mill Rate: A rate set each year by the municipality. It is determined by the total amount of tax dollars the municipality must collect from its property owners to pay for the municipal services and education provided.

Municipality: A city, borough, town, township, village, county, or region, with local self-government. It allows residents of a specific geographic area to provide services of common interest.

Municipal Council: A group of people elected by a municipality's voters to make choices on their behalf about the provision of municipal services.

Ontario Building Code: Standards for materials and design which all building construction and renovation must meet.

Polling List: A list of eligible voters.

Polling Place: The place where people vote. For example, schools, community centres, churches etc.

Property Assessment: A value assigned to the property based on a percentage of the dollar value of the property. The value is determined by a provincial assessor and used to calculate property taxes.

Property Standards By-Law: A by-law requiring buildings to be kept in a good state of repair and properties to be kept clear of debris for the health and safety of those who use them.

Property Tax: A collection of money from each property owner in the municipality to pay for the portion of services the municipality provides that cannot be paid for through grants from the province or user fees.

Public Utilities Commission: A commission elected to oversee the provision of electricity and in some cases, water. It also sets local rates. It is sometimes called a Hydro or Hydro-Electric Commission.

Reeve: The head of council in a village or township elected at large. Some towns, villages and townships also have a deputy reeve.

Regional Municipality: In ten areas of Ontario, county government has been replaced by regional government. Regional municipalities have authority over certain functions in all municipalities within their boundaries.

Returning Officer: The person responsible for conducting a local election. The returning officer, usually the municipal clerk, ensures an election is conducted fairly.

School Board: An elected body to oversee the provision of education in the area under the board's jurisdiction. The school board oversee's the building and maintenance of schools, the hiring of teachers and other staff, authorizes educational programs and approves textbooks. School boards are also called "Boards of Education."

Town: A mid-sized urban municipality with a population of between about 2,000 and 15,000.

Township: A form of municipality designed for rural areas. A township usually has a population of 1,000.

Trustees: Elected members of a school board or board of education.

Village: The smallest type of urban municipality with a minimum population of approximately 500.

Warden: The head of county council selected annually from among its members.

Wards: Geographic areas into which a municipality is divided for the purpose of electing members of council and school trustees.

Zoning By-Law: A by-law dividing the municipality into smaller areas called zones and setting out the ways in which the land within the zone can be used.